D0801857

THE
Little Book
OF
CELTIC BLESSINGS

In the same series

THE
Little Book
— OF —
CELTIC
BLESSINGS

compiled by
Caitlín Matthews

ELEMENT
Shaftesbury, Dorset ◆ Rockport, Massachusetts
Melbourne, Victoria

© *Element Books Limited 1994*
© *Text compilation Caitlín Matthews*

Published in Great Britain in 1994 by
ELEMENT BOOKS LIMITED
Shaftesbury, Dorset

Published in the USA in 1994 by
ELEMENT BOOKS INC.
PO Box 830, Rockport, MA 01966

Published in Australia in 1994 by
ELEMENT BOOKS LIMITED
and distributed by
Penguin Books Australia Limited,
487 Maroondah Highway, Ringwood, Victoria 3144

Reprinted 1995 and 1997

Front and back cover:
photograph reproduced by permission of
ET Archive
Designed and created by:
The Bridgewater Book Company / Ron Bryant-Funnell
Textual photographs by Sarah Bentley

Printed and bound in Great Britain by Cambus Litho, Scotland

British Library Cataloguing in Publication data available

Library of Congress Cataloging in Publication data available

ISBN 1-85230-564-9

CONTENTS

From the Wells of Life

This book brings together blessings, praises and prayers drawn from the Celtic world. The Celtic peoples share a common tradition of blessing with their Indo-European cousins, the Hindus. Each action, thought or intention is *sained*, made holy by blessing. Blessing is a consecration, an inclusion of the mundane within the sacred that confers grace and protection. Blessing allows whatever is blessed to fully realize its innate potential.

Currently, there is much disillusionment with narrow and unchangeable doctrines which lack respect for creation and for the spiritual needs of other living beings. Many people have turned to the inspiration of Celtic Christianity and its earlier pre-Christian tradition to provide a fresh and more inclusive approach to spiritual life, to find again a belonging in the web of life.

The extracts here are drawn from a variety of sources, ancient, medieval and nineteenth century, reflecting the ongoing Celtic concern with hallowing daily life: with the family and the

changing seasons, with affairs of daily life and
the soul's circuit, with the wide world and the
opportunities and dangers that may be
encountered therein. Encompassing all matters
is the concern to mend, unite and heal
whatever is disconnected with the interwoven
web of life, and to be personally and actively
aware of that unity.

The ancient dedication to the threefold
manifestation of the spirit recurs throughout
these blessings: whether it be the Holy Trinity
of Christianity, the earlier threefold of heaven,
earth and sea, or the triple aspects of the
Goddess, Brighid. This triplicity is mirrored in
the family of mother, father and child as well as
in the creative processes of conception,
creation and exposition. This underlying
framework of the Sacred Three supports,
satisfies and demarks all life in a protective
triple spiral.

We no longer live in traditional ways, but we
still need to bless, encourage or protect. When
stark need strikes, sharp as hunger or cold, we
need no priest to utter a blessing – the words
well up from our heart's depth unaided. If you

need a blessing for a specific purpose not covered here, then you are encouraged to draw upon your own needs and derive inspiration from this book to create your own. Blessing brings its own gift and arrives without formality. Blessing need not be loud and ostentatious. We bless quietly and with good intention those things and people whom we love and wish well.

Blessing can also serve to disconnect us from the invasive fibres of jealousy, hatred or enmity and teach us the way of harmlessness. With people whom we regard as difficult, adversarial or challenging we can disconnect the behaviour from the person, bless their soul and not their action.

Blessing is the essential lubricant of life, a deep thankfulness which bubbles up without stint from the well of mercy. May these benedictions reunite you with the simple gifts which nurture all life!

CAITLÍN MATTHEWS

The Home and Family

BLESSING FOR A NEW HOUSE

A blessing upon your new home,
  A blessing upon your new hearth,
A blessing upon your new dwelling,
  Upon your newly-kindled fire.

A blessing upon your tallest grass,
  A blessing upon your fruitful partner,
A blessing upon your growing son/s,
  Upon your growing daughter/s.

A blessing upon the household's helpers,
  A blessing upon the children yet unborn,
A blessing upon the wise parents,
  Upon your occupation.

A blessing upon your goods and income,
  A blessing upon your kith and kin,
A blessing upon you in light or darkness,
  Each day and night of your lives. [1]

BLESSING FOR THE CHILDREN

O Thou, to whom to love and to be are one, hear my faith-cry for them who are more thine than mine. Give each of them what is best for each. I cannot tell what it is. But Thou knowest. I only ask Thou love them and keep them with the loving and keeping Thou didst show to Mary's Son and Thine. [2]

BLESSING FOR HEARTH-KEEPERS

*B*righid of the Mantle, encompass us,
    Lady of the Lambs, protect us,
Keeper of the Hearth, kindle us.
    Beneath your mantle, gather us,
And restore us to memory.

Mothers of our mother,
    Foremothers strong,
Guide our hands in yours,
    Remind us how
To kindle the hearth,

To keep it bright,
To preserve the flame.
    Your hands upon ours,
Our hands within yours,
    To kindle the light,
Both day and night.

The Mantle of Brighid about us,
    The Memory of Brighid within us,
The Protection of Brighid keeping us
    From harm, from ignorance, from
        heartlessness,
This day and night,
    From dawn till dark,
From dark till dawn. [3]

Brighid is the Irish saint whose cult draws strongly upon the
Celtic Goddess of the same name; as hearth-keeper, she is
venerated throughout the Celtic world.

TWO BLESSINGS FOR HOSPITALITY

O King of stars!
Whether my house be dark or bright,
Never shall it be closed against any one,
Lest Christ close His house against me,

If there be a guest in your house
And you conceal aught from him.
'Tis not the guest that will be without it,
but Jesus, Mary's Son. [4]

I saw a stranger yestreen,
I put food in the eating place,
drink in the drinking place,
music in the listening place,
and in the sacred name of the Triune,
He blessed myself and my house,
my cattle and my dear ones,
and the lark said in her song
often, often, often
goes the Christ in the stranger's guise. [5]

BLESSING ON THE FIRE
AT NIGHT

I *smoor* the hearth,
As Mary smoors it;
The vigilance of Brighid and Mary
Be upon the fire and upon the floor
And over the whole household.

Who stands on the grass outside?
Sun-bright Mary and her Son,
The mouth of God requested, the angel of
   God spoke;
Angels of promise guard the hearth
Until bright day visits the fire.[6]

To *smoor* the fire is to bank it in for the night with turfs of peat,
so it may be raised in the morning. This blessing can be used
for extinguishing any fire at night.

BLESSING OF THE THREE

The Sacred Three
My fortress be
Encircling me.
Come and be round
My hearth, my home.

Fend Thou my kin
And every sleeping thing within
From scathe, from sin.
Thy care our peace
Through mid of night
To light's release.[7]

The Seasons

THE BLESSING OF THE ELEMENTS

I arise today
Through the strength of heaven:
Light of sun,
Radiance of moon,
Splendour of fire,
Speed of lightning,
Swiftness of wind,
Depth of sea,
Stability of earth,
Firmness of rock.[8]

BLESSING OF THE SEASONS

Autumn is a good time for visiting:
During its short days there is work for all.
See the dappled fawns among the hinds,
Sheltering in the red bracken;
See the stags run from the round hills
At the belling of the deer-tribe.
There are sweet acorns in the high woods,
Cornstalks are king over the brown earth.
A pallisade of brambles guards
the ruined rath,
The hard ground is enriched
by a treasury of fruit.
Profuse the hazel-nuts from the ancient hedge-
trees.

Black is the season of deep winter,
The margins of the world are storm-crested.
Sad are the birds of every meadow,
Lamenting the harsh winter's clamour,
All save ravens gorged on blood.

Winter – rough-black, dark-smoked,
cold-flinted.
Dogs splinter the cracking bones,
Cauldrons sit on fires at the dark day's end.

Raw and chill is icy spring,
Cold sits on every wind.
On the sodden pool, ducks cry out,
Eager is the harsh-shrieking crane.
From the wilderness, wolves scent
morning prey,
Birds rise from meadowed nest,
Many are the wild things of the wood,
That they flee from out of the greening earth.

Good is the season of peaceful summer;
The council of the trees gather together,
A band unshaken by the whistling wind,
A green gathering in the sheltered woods;
Eddies swirl the stream,
Good is the warm turf under us.[9]

*

BLESSING OF THE SEASONAL SAINTS

Saints of Four Seasons,
Saints of the Year.
Loving, I pray to you; longing, I say to you:
Save me from angers, *dreeings*, and dangers!
(sorrows)
Saints of Four Seasons,
Saints of the Year.

Saints of the Green Springtime,
Saints of the Year.
Patraic and Grighair, Brighid be near.
My last breath gather with God's Foster Father.
Saints of the Green Springtime,
Saints of the Year.

Saints of Gold Summer,
Saints of the Year.
Poesy wingeth me, fancy far bringeth me,
Guide ye me on to Mary's Sweet Son.
Saints of Gold Summer,
Saints of the Year.

Saints of Red Autumn,
Saints of the Year.
Lo! I am cheery, Michil and Mary,
Open wide Heaven to my soul bereaven.
Saints of Red Autumn,
Saints of the Year.

Saints of Grey Winter,
Saints of the Year.
Outside God's Palace fiends wait in malice –
Let them not win my soul going in.
Saints of Grey Winter,
Saints of the Year.

Saints of Four Seasons,
Saints of the Year.
Waking or sleeping, to my grave creeping,
Life in its Night, hold me God's light.
Saints of Four Seasons,
Saints of the Year.[10]

Daily Life

BLESSING BEFORE LEAVING HOME FOR WORK

This day is your love-gift to me.
This dawn... I take it from your hand.
Make me busy in your service
throughout its hours,
yet not so busy that I cannot
sing a happy song.
And may the south wind blow its
tenderness through my heart
so that I bear myself gently towards all.
And may the sunshine of it
pass into my thoughts,
so that each shall be a picture of your
thought, noble and right.[11]

BLESSING IN DISSATISFACTION

Many a time I wish I were other than I am.
  I weary of the solemn tide;
    of the little fields;
      of this brooding isle.

I long to be rid of the weight of duty
    and to have my part in ampler life.

O Thou, who art wisdom and pity both,
    set me free from the lordship of desire.

Help me to find my happiness
in my acceptance of what is my purpose:
  in friendly eyes;
    in work well done;
      in quietness born of trust,
        and, most of all,
in the awareness of your presence
    in my spirit.[12]

BLESSINGS BEFORE AND AFTER MEALS

Be with me, O God, at the breaking of bread,
  Be with me, O God, at the end of my meal;
May no morsel of my body's partaking
  Add to my soul's freight.[13]

Thanks to you, O God,
  Praise to you, O God,
  Honour to you, O God,
  For all you have given me.

You have given me bodily existence
  To win me earthly food,
  Grant me also immortal life
  To reveal your glory.

Grant me grace throughout my living,
  Grant me life at my death's coming;
Be with me, O God, as breath casts off,
God, be with my soul in the high seas.

In the casting off of breath,
Be with my soul in the high seas.
God guide my soul through the narrows,
When I cross the deep flood. [14]

BLESSING FOR A HAND-MADE GARMENT

May you wear the garment to shreds!
May you wear the garment to tatters!
May you wear the garment
With food and music
In every place
As I would wish:

With confidence,
With health,
With friends,
With love,
With the grace of the Threefold Spirit. [15]

ANGELIC BLESSING ON SLEEPING

May the angels watch me
As I lie down to sleep.
May angels guard me
As I sleep alone.

Uriel be at my feet,
Ariel be at my back,
Gabriel be at my head,
Raphael be at my side.

Michael protect my soul
With the strong shield of love.
And the healing Son of Mary
Touch my eyes with blessedness. [16]

BLESSING OF THE
GUARDIAN ANGEL

O Being of Brightness, Friend of Light,
   From the Blessed Realms of Grace,
Gently encircle me, sweetly enclosing me,
Guarding my soul-shrine from harm this
                    day/night.

Keep me from anguish,
   Keep me from danger,
Encircle my voyage over the seas.
   A light will you lend me,
   To keep and defend me,
O Beautiful Being, O Guardian this night.

Be a guiding star above me,
   Illuminate each rock and tide,
Guide my ship across the waters,
   To the waveless harbourside. [17]

The Soul's Journey

BLESSING FOR A NEW-BORN CHILD

A small wave for your form

A small wave for your voice

A small wave for your speech

A small wave for your means

A small wave for your generosity

A small wave for your appetite

A small wave for your wealth

A small wave for your life

A small wave for your health.

Nine waves of grace upon you.

Waves of the Giver of Health. [18]

BLESSING FOR A BRIDE AND GROOM

Length of life and sunny days,
and may your souls not go homewards
till your own child falls in love! [19]

BLESSING FOR A LOVER

You are the star of each night,
You are the brightness of every morning,
You are the story of each guest,
You are the report of every land.

No evil shall befall you, On hill nor bank,
In field or valley, On mountain or in glen.

Neither above nor below, Neither in sea
Nor on shore,
In skies above, Nor in the depths.

You are the kernel of my heart,
You are the face of my sun,
You are the harp of my music,
You are the crown of my company. [20]

BLESSING ON A YOUNG PERSON'S LEAVING HOME

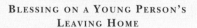

We bathe your palms
  In showers of wine,
In the crook of the kindling,
  In the seven elements,
In the sap of the tree,
  In the milk of honey,

We place nine pure, choice gifts
  In your clear beloved face:

The gift of form,
  The gift of voice,
The gift of fortune,
  The gift of goodness,
The gift of eminence,
  The gift of charity,
The gift of integrity,
  The gift of true nobility,
The gift of apt speech.

Dark is yonder town,
  Dark are those within,

You are the brown swan,
  Going within fearlessly,
Their hearts beneath your hand,
  Their tongues beneath your foot,
No word will they utter
  To do you ill.

You are a shade in the heat,
  You are a shelter in the cold,
You are eyes to the blind,
  You are a staff to the pilgrim,
You are an island in the sea,
  You are a stronghold upon land,
You are a well in the wasteland,
  You are healing to the sick.

You are the luck of every joy,
  You are the light of the sun's beams,
You are the door of lordly welcome,
  You are the pole star of guidance,
You are the step of the roe of the height,
  You are the step of the white-faced mare,
You are the grace of the swimming swan,
  You are the jewel in each mystery. [21]

BLESSING FOR THE SOUL'S RELEASE

You go home this night
to your home of winter,
To your home of autumn,
of spring and of summer;
You go home this night to your lasting home,
To your eternal bed, to your sound sleeping.

Sleep now, sleep, and so fade sorrow,
Sleep now, sleep, and so fade sorrow,
Sleep now, sleep, and so fade sorrow,
Sleep, my beloved, in the rock of the fold.

The sleep of seven lights upon you, my dear,
The sleep of seven joys upon you, my dear,
The sleep of seven slumbers upon you,
my dear.

Sleep, oh sleep in the quiet of quietness,
Sleep, oh sleep in the way of guidance,
Sleep, oh sleep in the love of all loving. [22]

The Wide World

TWO BLESSINGS OF THE SUN

O King of the sun's brightness,
who alone has knowledge of our purpose,
be with us every day,
be with us every night,
be with us every night and day,
be with us every day and night. [23]

Welcome to you, sun of the seasons'
  turning,
In your circuit of the high heavens;
Strong are your steps on the unfurled heights,
Glad Mother are you to the constellations.

You sink down into the ocean of want,
Without defeat and without scathe;
You rise up on the peaceful wave
Like a queen in her maidenhood's flower. [24]

Note: Among the Gaels, the sun is feminine.

BLESSING OF THE MOON

When I see the new moon,
  It becomes me to lift mine eye,
It becomes me to bend my knee,
  It becomes me to bow my head.

Giving thee praise, thou moon of guidance,
  That I have seen thee again,
That I have seen the new moon,
  The lovely leader of the way.

Many a one has passed beyond
  In the time between the two moons,
Though I am still enjoying earth,
  Thou moon of moons and of blessings. [25]

Blessing on Setting Forth

May the road rise to meet you.
May the wind always be at your back.
May the sun shine warm upon your face,
The rains fall soft upon your fields;
And, until we meet again, may
God hold you in the palm of his hand. [26]

Blessing for a Journey

Bless to me, O God,
    the earth beneath my foot.
Bless to me, O God, the path whereon I go.
Bless to me, O God, the thing of my desire.
Thou evermore of evermore,
    Bless Thou to me my rest . . .
As thou wast before at my life's beginning, be
thou so again at my journey's end.
As thou wast besides at my soul's shaping,
Father, be thou too, at my journey's close. [27]

BLESSING FOR ANIMALS

I say the blessing of Brighid
That she placed about her calf and her cows,
About her horses and her goats,
About her sheep and her lambs:

Each day and night,
In cold and heat,
Each day and night,
In light and darkness:

Keep them from marsh,
Keep them from rocks,
Keep them from pits,
Keep them from banks;

Keep them from harm,
Keep them from jealousy,
Keep them from spell,
From North to South;

Keep them from poison,
From East and West,
Keep them from envy,
And from all harmful intentions. [28]

The Circle of Safety

BLESSING OF PROTECTION

To Christ the seed,
  To Christ the harvest:
To the barn of Christ
  May we be brought.

  To Christ the sea,
    To Christ the fish:
  In the nets of Christ
    May we be caught.

    From birth to age,
      From age to death:
    Your two arms, Christ,
      About us safe.

      From death to ending,
        Not ended but regrown:
      In the Paradise of Grace
        May we be transplanted. [29]

BLESSING OF THE DRUIDIC CIRCLE

Grant, O God, Thy Protection,
And in protection, strength,
And in strength, understanding,
And in understanding, perception of justice,
And in perception of justice, the love of it,
And in the love of it, the love of all Life,
and in all Life, to love God,
God and all goodness. [30]

BLESSING FOR GUIDANCE

Great *Bran*, whose head sang for his followers
for years unnumbered upon the Island of
Gwales in Caer Siddi, you who were a bridge to
your people, and who gave shape and purpose
to the acts of those who followed you, I ask that
you grant us the light of your blessing and that
you guide our footsteps on the paths of
peacefulness. [31]

Bran the Blessed is an ancestral British deity who sacrificed his
earthly life in order to become an otherworldly protector of the
land.

The Indwelling Spirit of Peace

TWO BLESSINGS OF THE THREE

The blessing-help of the Three upon my
   wishing,
The blessing-help of the Three upon my
   willing,
The blessing-help of the Three upon my
   walking,
and upon my knees that they may never
   weaken. [32]

The Father, the Son and the Holy Spirit,
May the Three in One be with us day and night.
Whether in the depths of the sea or on the
   mountainside,
May our Mother be with us, her arm around
   our heads. [33]

A Druidic Blessing for Unity

We swear by peace and love to stand
  Heart to heart and hand in hand.
Mark, O Spirit, and hear us now,
  Confirming this our Sacred Vow. [34]

Blessing to Heal a Sprain or Any Disunity

Bride went out
  One morning early,
With her two horses;
  One broke its leg
With much ado.
  What was apart
She put together
  Bone to bone,
Flesh to flesh,
  Sinew to sinew,
Vein to vein;
  As she healed that
May we heal this. [35]

BLESSING OF HEALING

I wish healing upon you,
The healing of Mary with me,
Mary, Michael and Brighid
    Be with me all three.

Your pain and sickness
    Be in the earth's depths,
Be upon the grey stones,
    For they are enduring.

Fly with the birds of the air,
Fly with the wasps of the hill,
Swim with the sea-going whale,
    For they are swiftest.

Be upon the clouds of the sky,
    For they are the rainiest,
Be upon the river's current
    Cascading to the sea. [36]

BLESSING FOR ANY FRIEND

Power of raven be yours,
Power of eagle be yours,
Power of the *Fianna*.

Power of storm be yours,
Power of moon be yours,
Power of sun.

Power of sea be yours,
Power of land be yours,
Power of heaven.

Goodness of sea be yours,
Goodness of earth be yours,
Goodness of heaven.

Each day be joy to you,
No day be sad to you,
Honour and tenderness. [37]

The *Fianna* were the troop of warriors led by the
Irish hero, Fionn MacCumhail.

BLESSING OF PEACE-HEALING

Deep peace I breathe into you,
O weariness, here:
O ache, here!
Deep peace, a soft white dove to you;
Deep peace, a quiet rain to you;
Deep peace, an ebbing wave to you!
Deep peace, red wind of the east from you;
Deep peace, grey wind of the west to you;
Deep peace, dark wind of the north from you;
Deep peace, blue wind of the south to you!
Deep peace, pure red of the flame to you;
Deep peace, pure white of the moon to you;
Deep peace, pure green of the grass to you;
Deep peace, pure brown of the earth to you;
Deep peace, pure grey of the dew to you,
Deep peace, pure blue of the sky to you!
Deep peace of the running wave to you,
Deep peace of the flowing air to you,
Deep peace of the quiet earth to you,

Deep peace of the sleeping stones to you,
Deep peace of the Yellow Shepherd to you,
Deep peace of the Wandering
    Shepherdess to you,
Deep peace of the Flock of Stars to you,
Deep peace of the Son of Peace to you,
Deep peace from the heart of Mary to you,
And from Bridget of the Mantle,
Deep peace, deep peace! [38]

Sources

1. *Beannachadh Taighe*, trans. C. Matthews from *Carmina Gadelica*, ed. Alexander Carmichael, vol.3, Scottish Academic Press, 1972.

2. Alistair MacLean, *Hebridean Altars*, Moray Press, 1937.

3. 'Invocation of Brighid' by C. Matthews from *Power of Raven* by Noragh Jones, Floris Books, 1994.

4. Trans. Kuno Meyer, *Ancient Irish Poetry*, Constable, 1913.

5. From The Book of Cerne, in *A Pilgrim's Manual*, Paulinus Press, 1985.

6. *Reannnaladh Smualadh*, trans. C. Matthews, from *Carmina Gadelica*, ed. Alexander Carmichael, vol.1, Scottish Academic Press, 1972.

7. MacLean.

8. Meyer.

9. Anon. Irish Poem of 11th century, trans. C. Matthews.

10. Irish litany trans. P.J.McCall in *The Poem-Book of the Gael*, ed. Eleanor Hull. Chatto & Windus, 1912.

11. MacLean.

12. Ibid.

13. *Buidheachas Bithidh*, trans. C. Matthews, from *Carmina Gadelica*, vol 3.

14. Ibid.

15. *Basradh*, trans. C. Matthews from *Carmina Gadelica*, vol. 4, ed. A. Carmichael, Oliver & Boyd, 1941.

16. *Laighim am Leabaidh*, trans. C. Matthews from *Carmina Gadelica*, vol.1.

17. Matthews, C., *Celtic Book of the Dead*, St Martin's Press, 1991.

18. *Or an Tonnaidh* by Mhairi nic Neill, trans. by C. Matthews from *Carmina Gadelica*, vol.3.

19. Trad. Irish blessing, trans. C. Matthews.

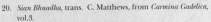

20. *Sian Bhuadha*, trans. C. Matthews, from *Carmina Gadelica*, vol.3.

21. Trad. Gaelic from *Ladies of the Lake*, C. & J. Matthews, Aquarian, 1991.

22. *Sian Bhuadha*, trans. C. Matthews.

23. Trad. Irish blessing, trans. C. Matthews.

24. Trad. West Highland, trans. C. Matthews.

25. F. Marian MacNeil, *The Silver Bough*, William MacClelland, 1956.

26. Traditional.

27. Alexander Donald's prayer, from *A Pilgrim's Manual*, Paulinus Press, 1985.

28. *Sian Seilbh*, trans. C. Matthews, from *Carmina Gadelica*, vol. 4.

29. Trad. Irish hymn, trans. C. Matthews.

30. Gorsedd Prayer, Dillwyn Miles, *The Royal National Eisteddfod of Wales*, Christopher Davis, 1977.

31. John Matthews, 'Invocation of Bran the Blessed' from *Paths to Peace*, ed. J. Matthews, Rider, 1992.

32. Trad. Irish blessing, trans. C. Matthews.

33. Ibid.

34. Trad. Druidic vow, from Philip Carr-Gomm, *The Druid Way*, Element, 1993.

35. *Eolas an t-Snamh*, trans. C. Matthews, from *Carmina Gadelica*, vol.2.

36. *Eolas na Glacaich*, trans. C. Matthews, from *Carmina Gadelica*, vol.4.

37. *Durachd* by Mary Mackintosh, trans. C. Matthews, from *Carmina Gadelica*, vol.3.

38. Fiona MacLeod, *Under the Dark Star*, William Heinemann, 1912.

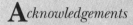Acknowledgements

The publishers would like to thank the following for
permission to reproduce their illustrations:
The Bridgeman Art Library – pages 4, 40
E.T. Archive, British Library – page 10
E.T. Archive, Trinity College Dublin – pages 2, 12
E.T. Archive, Victoria & Albert Museum – page 14